Paper Thoughts

Aubrey Monson

BookLeaf Publishing

Presentation by *BookLeaf Publishing*

Web: www.bookleafpub.com

E-mail: info@bookleafpub.com

ISBN: 9789357213271

First edition 2023

When Did It Change

When did battleship
Turn into he said she said;
Everyone firing cannons,
Hoping to hit their mark?

When were words laced with acid
In the hope that they sting;
Lashing out at the smallest thing,
To take the biggest bite?

When did common pastimes
Become exclusive and demeaning,
Leaving bruises on souls
To compile a painting?

When did we realize
That it was too late,
And how can we go back
To a simple game of battleship?

For You

If I could I would give you the world.
If you told me you loved the stars,
Darling I would pull them from the skies
To give to you.
I would bring you dancing constellations,
And cover you in stardust.
I would paint your name in the sky,
And take you to the moon.
If you told me the ocean intrigued you,
I would swim with you to the depths,
Finding anemones and fish of all colors.
I would find you pearls,
And give you treasures untold.
Darling if you told me anything,
And I could give it to you, I would.
Because all I want in this life
Is you.

To Feel

In a world of chaos and confusion,
In a generation of heartbreak and hostility,
In a community of fake smiles,
We become acrobats.
Bending into the shapes that people want to see,
Performing tricks that they can't comprehend.
We become artists,
Painting perfect views,
Leaving splotches on the floor where we stood.
We become athletes, actors, advocates,
We become anything we are told to be
Just to please a crowd
That gives false praise,
And empty compliments.
Just to feel full,
When we are dry to the bone.
Just to feel anything at all,
Even if it isn't real.

Heard It On The News

You heard it on the news,
Like a deathly plague.
The sirens in your heart went off
As they listed off crimes
We all seem to commit.

You heard it on the news,
A corrupted society,
Taking any means necessary
To get what it wants.

You heard it on the news,
Each day it gets worse,
Each day people stop caring.

You heard it on the news,
And you could see it in you.

You heard it on the news.

Fear

Fear of the unknown,
Fear of repeating the past;
Fear kept me from you.

Stages of Growing

We crawl then walk then run
We babble before we talk,
We paddle before we swim,
We learn to grow in stages.

It seems we hit a point
Where we stop growing.

We think we've peaked,
We have grown all we can.
We seek the spotlight or
We hide in plain sight.

Desperate for approval,
Critical when it comes.

We crave success but
We fear trying.
We fear failing so
We stop where we are.

Until it hits that we
Ran then walked then crawled.

The Jester

I was just the jester
Providing entertainment for the king-
You were the king.
Making me dance and act and sing.
Poking fun at the tune of my song,
Calling me at your leisure
To perform another trick.

You called, and you called, and you called,
And I came, I came, I came.
I was just the jester,
Performing for you, the king.
Wrecking myself for you,
Hoping you enjoyed my company,
Giving genuine smiles to please you.

I came and I came and I came,
Each time bringing something new.
Trying to impress you,
Trying to win your affection,
Hoping it would last.
But you were the king,
And I was just the jester.

Hands

They are rough
From working hard.
They are soft
When they pull me in.
They are comfort
When I need it most.

Your hands keep me warm
On a winters day.
They provide and protect
From everything bad in the world.
Your hands tell me
I am home.

Information Overload

You get lost in the tumult of opinions,
And the thrum of voices.
Turning this way and that
To find a reliable source.
You get thrown in with the mix,
Transforming with the masses,
Unable to keep track
Of the ways they change you.
Your guard starts to slip
As you lose your balance,
Steadying yourself
On the information they feed you.
You run in circles,
Trying to retain a sense of reality,
Until you're staring in the mirror-
A shattered reflection of who you used to be.

Stoney Foundations

We go through life
Picking stones from our path
As we go.
Putting them together
To patch up a future,
Picturing a sturdy foundation
With beautiful landscape.
Unprepared for the moss
That grows through the cracks,
Unprepared for the cold
That seeps through the walls,
Breaking in places we didn't expect.
We form a future
With stones in our pockets,
Expecting it to be indestructible,
Crumbling when we realize
No number of stones
Can build the future we want.

Chasing Dreams

I was a dream catcher,
Or rather a dream chaser.
Until the world stomped out my spark,
Telling me it was useless.
That as I chased,
My dreams would keep on running,
Making it impossible for me to catch them.
I didn't listen at first,
But I guess I grew into it.
I accepted the stories of the world,
And stopped chasing my dreams.

I was a dream chaser,
Never afraid of getting lost.
Trusting in myself
To find my way.
I ran until I could run no more,
Losing my breath as I went,
But finding it in my hope.
Then one day I stopped running,
And it seems my dreams kept going.
I now find myself searching,
Grasping for a way to catch my dreams.

I Can Be

With you I can dance on tabletops,
Or fall down a flight of stairs.
I can be anything I want to be,
Even if I'm afraid and insecure.
You hold me together at the seams
Until I can stitch myself up,
Because you know I'd hate for you to do it.
I like my independence,
Neatly next to my dependence on you.
You keep me calm
When there's a whirlwind inside me.
On quiet nights you focus on me,
And make me laugh so hard I can't breathe.
I'm on the forefront of your mind,
And the tip of your tongue,
Just as you are on mine.
I wear my heart on my sleeve,
Only allowing you to see
The parts of me I tried so hard to hide.
Because with you,
I can be anything I want to be.

You And I

I lived a lifetime of peace,
And online wars.
You lived a lifetime of wars,
And community peace.

You never really talked about it,
I always seem to.
You wanted independence,
I want social approval.

I see things fall apart,
You already have.
I get scared for the future,
You feel no need.

You gave me a good life,
I recognize that now.
You did all you could,
I see it was enough.

Lost In The Current

Our story runs like rushing water,
Beautiful to the senses,
But dangerous to the soul,
Too easy to get swept away in the current.

We run by the wayside,
Kicking droplets of water as we go.
Stopping to skip rocks
And watch the current flow.

We decide to swim,
Jumping in without a second thought.
Splashing and laughing,
Not thinking about getting caught.

Not worried when we are,
Until we see the sun set,
Realizing we are lost,
And all we feel is wet.

We bob up and down,
Reaching for the sand.
But true to its nature,
It slips through our hands.

It was easy to get swept away in the current,
And dangerous to the soul,
But beautiful to the senses;
Our story ran like rushing water.

Knock Despite The Fear

We knock and we knock,
Not knowing what's behind the door,
Afraid of what we'll find,
Terrified of what we'll miss.

So we approach
With timid feet,
And shaking hands,
But sturdy determination.

Glancing back at what we've left,
Then setting our gaze forward
We raise our fist,
And knock.

Our World

We work together,
Creating a dream like world,
Just for you and I.

Haunted

You say that you're fine,
And tuck it inside.
You pretend you're okay,
That you don't have scars
Lining the walls of your mind.
There are days that you break,
When the memories claw their way out,
Creating new wounds,
Shattering you yet again.
You say that you're fine,
And pray we can't see
Through your lies.
You pretend you're okay,
But there's not a day
You're not haunted.

A Memory

A memory, knocking at my door,
Begging to come inside.
A memory,
Continuing to lure me in.
A memory,
Distant, but pulsing with life.

Goodbye

I wasn't ready to say goodbye when I did.
I wasn't ready to let you go.
I didn't think it would be the last time
I would see you, would feel you, would hear
you.

I wasn't ready to say goodbye,
But I did.
I said goodbye,
Even if you couldn't hear it.

I wasn't ready to let you go,
But I had to.
It wasn't in my power
To make you stay.

I didn't think it would be the last time,
When I got on that plane
To face my next adventure,
I thought you would be here when I got home.

I thought I would see you, feel you, hear you,
At least one more time.
I wasn't ready for you to become a memory.
But you did.

Our Demons

We all have demons we battle,
Pretending that we don't.
But they claw, and bite, and sting,
And sometimes they slip past our defense,
Taking the face we hold,
Stealing our skin like it was always theirs.
Sometimes we have no fight left.
We give up and we give in,
Letting them take over everything we claimed to
be.
We all have demons,
Even if we pretend we don't.
We all have demons,
And try as we might to free ourselves,
They have an eternal grip.
We all have demons,
And we always will.

Till Forever Falls Apart

The song said until forever falls apart,
And though we weren't the ones dancing
I looked to you to find a rhythm.
You kissed my head,
Swaying to the music,
And it felt like the song was written for us.
I'll love you until forever falls apart,
And even then I'll find a way
To fix up everything that broke.
Restoring our forever,
Creating an eternity with you,
And even that will never be enough.
There will never be a way to say
How much or how long I'll love you.
So I guess until forever falls apart
Is as close as I'll come,
Knowing I will never let
Our forever fall apart.

www.ingramcontent.com/pod-product-compliance
Lightning Source LLC
Chambersburg PA
CBHW051721130826
49812CB00034B/1294
9789357213271